Caring for Lawns

Caring for Lawns

WRITER
Mike Bowker

PHOTOGRAPHER
Barry Shapiro

ILLUSTRATOR
James Balkovek

LAWN & GARDEN

Acquisition, Development and Production Services by BMR, Corte Madera, CA

Acquisition: JACK JENNINGS, BOB DOLEZAL

Series Concept: BOB DOLEZAL

Developmental Editing: BOB DOLEZAL

Photographic Director: ALAN COPELAND

Cover Design: KAREN EMERSON

Cover Photo: BARRY SHAPIRO

Interior Art: JAMES BALKOVEK

North American Map: RON HILDEBRAND

Copy Editing: NAOMI LUCKS, JANET REED

Proofreader: TOM HASSETT

Typography and Page Layout: BARBARA GELFAND

Index: SYLVIA COATES

Horticulturist and Site Scout: PEGGY HENRY

Color Separations: PREPRESS ASSEMBLY INCORPORATED

Printing and Binding: PENDELL PRINTING INC.

Production Management: THOMAS E. DORSANEO, JANE RYAN

Film: FUJI VELVIA

Special thanks to Rich and Cam Martindale, Sonoma, CA for the cover site.

Additional photo credits: Cynthia Ash, pages 54–55, for Fairy ring, Fusarium patch, Powdery mildew, Red thread, Slime mold. Philip O. Larsen, pages 54–55, for Rust, Stripe smut, Anthracnose, Leaf spot, Patch problems. Ward Stienstra, pages 54–55, for Pythium blight.

Library of Congress Catalog-in-Publication Data
Bowker, Michael.
  Caring for lawns / writer, Michael Bowker; photographer, Barry Shapiro; illustrator, James Balkovek.
    p. cm.
  ISBN: 1-880281-04-X
  1. Lawns. I. Shapiro, Barry. II. Balkovek, James. III. Title.
[SB433.B69 1992]
635.9'647—dc20

92-26410
CIP

95   10   9   8   7   6   5   4   3

CARING FOR LAWNS

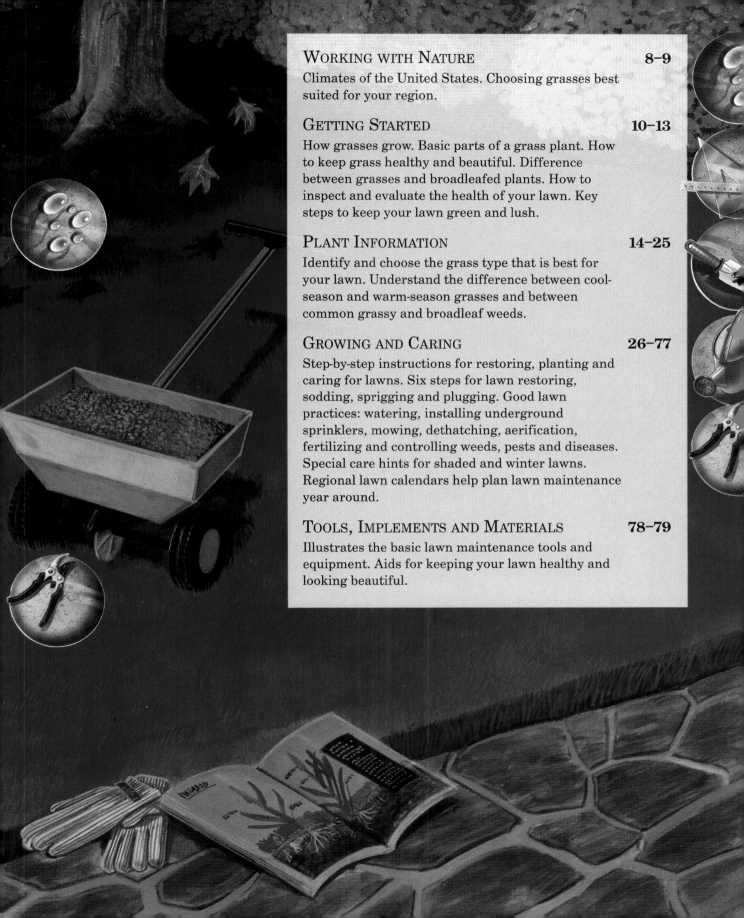

CLIMATE AND LAWN GRASSES

Choose the best grasses for your climate. Grass is divided into *cool-season* (grows in the cooler, northern climates, but withers in hot southern summers) or *warm-season* (flourishes in summer heat, but becomes dormant—turns brown—in chilly weather). A mix is often used in areas where summers are hot and winters are cold.

South

Hot, moist summers, cool winters. Choose bermudagrass, St. Augustinegrass or centipedegrass. Use tall fescue and Kentucky bluegrass in higher, cooler elevations.

Southwest

Hot, dry summers, mild winters. Pick bermudagrass, St. Augustinegrass or zoysia for lower elevations, buffalograss and perennial ryegrass in the higher elevations and winter overseeding.

Tropical

Wet and warm year around. In very wet areas, disease-tolerant carpetgrass is used. Bermudagrass, centipedegrass, bahiagrass and St. Augustinegrass also do well.

Mountain States, West Canada

Very cold winters, dry summers. Choose native grasses like buffalograss, crested wheatgrass and blue grama. For irrigated, protected areas use fescues and Kentucky bluegrass.

Northeast, East Canada

Wet, mild summers, cold winters. Use Kentucky bluegrass, fine fescues and perennial ryegrass.

Transition

Both cool-season and warm-season grasses are used in mixes. Neither can adapt year round. Fescues provide best result.

Midwest

Hot, humid summers, cold winters. Use bluegrass, perennial ryegrass and fescue.

Pacific Northwest

Cool, moist climate with moderate winters. Kentucky bluegrass and fine fescues do well.

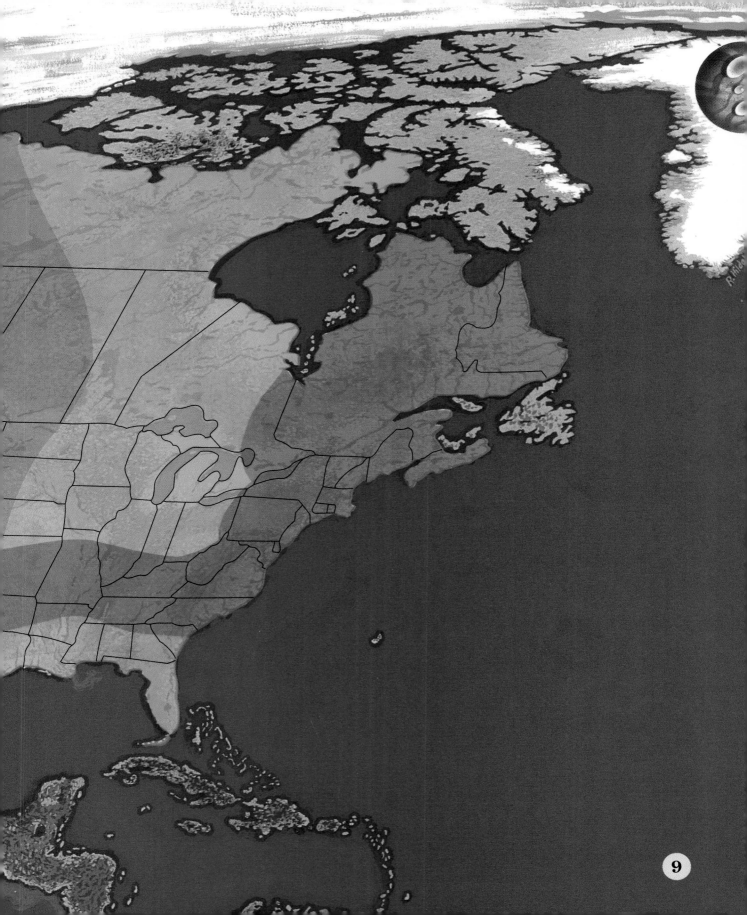

LAWN GRASSES

Plants are divided into two broad categories: *Monocotyledons*—grasses that emerge from the ground as a single blade—and *Dicotyledons*—broadleaf plants that poke from the soil as a pair of leaves.

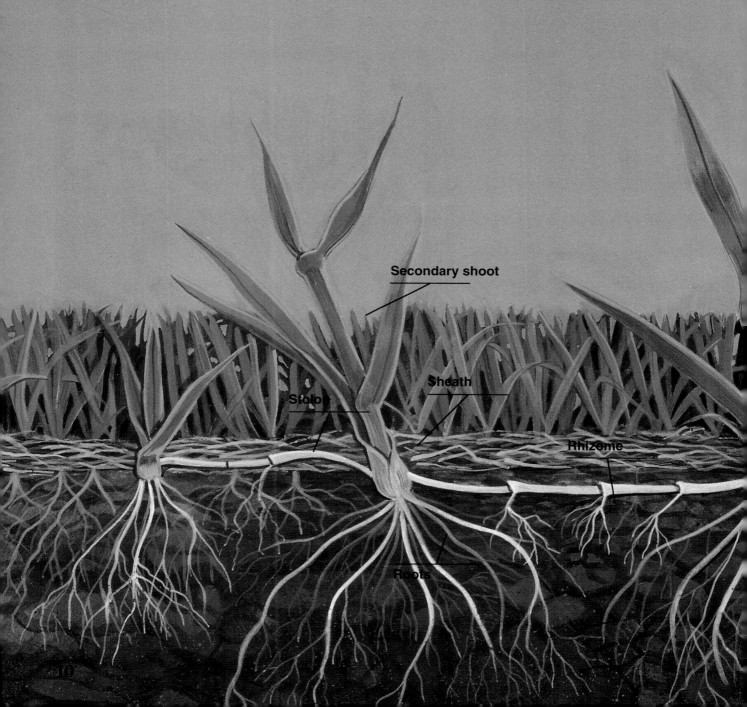

Secondary shoot

Sheath

Stolon

Rhizome

Roots

Blade

Internode

Collar

Node

Crown   **Thatch**

ABOUT LAWN GRASSES

Most of us grew up playing on lawns or ball fields. Few things are more nostalgic or pleasing than the smell of freshly-cut grass.

All grasses grow from seeds, spread underground from rhizomes, or put out runners called stolons that start secondary shoots. The most important part of all grasses is the crown, where the roots join the blades and sheath. Sometimes mowing too close or short damages the crown, killing the grass. This is called "scalping."

To grow and maintain a healthy lawn isn't difficult, but it does take some know-how. In lawns, grass plants are being asked to grow closer together than they normally would in nature so they require special attention. This includes growing the right type of grasses.

Gardeners use the difference between grasses and broadleaf plants to aid them in caring for their lawns. Because some weedkillers affect only broadleaf plants, it is possible to kill them without harming nearby lawn grasses.

The climate map (see pg. 8) helps guide you to the type of grasses that grow in your area. Look at each type of grass (see pg. 14). Each has features, uses and advantages that make it different than the others.

There are fine and coarse grasses, drought-tolerant varieties, types that require frequent, heavy fertilization or need little; and those that can be mowed close or allowed to grow several inches tall. Insect- and disease-tolerant varieties have also been developed.

11

INSPECTING AND EVALUATING YOUR LAWN

Many things affect your lawn's vigor and growth, including sunlight, slope and soil condition. Shaded lawns may need extra care, and water on sloped lawns should neither puddle nor run off too quickly. Check your lawn regularly for soil compaction, thatch buildup, weeds, pests, diseased and other special problems. Care differs from season to season depending on where you live.

Weeds are plants that grow where they aren't wanted. Weeds may be either narrowleaf (grasses) or broadleaf (non-grassy) plants.

Lift a 6–8 in. section of turf using a trowel or small shovel. Check for water penetration, root development and any soil or root pests.

PLANNING HEALTHY LAWNS

Keeping your lawn looking healthy and beautiful isn't difficult. All you need to do is water, fertilize and mow it regularly and inspect it from time to time to prevent little problems from becoming big ones.

Weeds (see pg. 22) and pests (see pg. 48) are two of the most common problems in most lawns. Weeds are usually easy to identify and most can be controlled by maintenance, by hand or chemical controls are available (see pg. 42) if needed. Although weeds can sprout up any time of the year, they are usually more aggressive during the spring and fall in areas with cooler climates. In areas with warmer climates, such as the Southern states and the Southwest, spring and summer are the times to look out for weeds. You can stay ahead of the weeds by inspecting your lawn every week or two, especially during those months when they are the most active in your lawn.

Also check for lawn pests such as insects during your inspections. They can be active year round, although they are usually inactive during winter in colder areas. Good lawn maintenance practices will help keep pests to a minimum, but at times you may have to treat your lawn to control them (see pg. 50).

Your periodic lawn inspections should also include a check for soil compaction and thatch buildup (see pg. 38), diseases (see pg. 54), and whether the turf is soaking up water evenly. (If puddling or rapid runoff occurs, you may want to regrade sections of your lawn.) Your lawn evaluations should also include a soil test (see pg. 26) about every other year to ensure that the nutrient level of your turf remains balanced.

CHOOSING GRASS TYPES
COOL-SEASON GRASSES

The right grass is the key to a beautiful, healthy and easily maintained lawn. These pages will help you identify your lawn grass and choose others. These are the cool-season grasses. Warm-season and native grasses follow. Some common lawn weeds are also shown.

Colonial Bentgrass

Agrostis tennuis

Not recommended. Fine-bladed and able to stand moderate wear. Requires light to average watering. Needs sun but may wither in extreme heat. Best along cool coastlines. Tolerates acidic (pH below 6.0) and infertile soils. Plant by seed in the fall or spring. (6.5 million seeds/lb. Recommend 1 lb./1,000 sq. ft. Germinates in 4–12 days. Mow 1/2–1 in. high.)

Creeping Bentgrass

Agrostis palustris

Not recommended. Fine-bladed, requires more water and is more sensitive to pests and fungal disease than colonial bentgrass. Takes a fair amount of wear, tolerates heat, handles more shade and has deep roots. Plant by seed in the fall or spring. (6.5 million seeds/lb. Recommend 1–2 lbs./1,000 sq. ft. Germinates in 4–12 days. Mow to 1/4–1/2 in. high.)

Kentucky Bluegrass

Poa pratensis

Most commonly planted cool-season grass. Withstands heavy foot traffic, cold winters; some varieties resist common pests and diseases. Grows best in full sun, though some varieties are adapted to part shade. Blades are blue-green and wide. Plant by seed or sod in fall or spring. (2.2 million seeds/lb. Recommend 2 lbs./1,000 sq. ft. Germinates in 6–30 days. Mow 1 1/2–2 in. high.)

Rough-Stalk, Rough Bluegrass

Poa trivialis

Lacks the toughness and cold tolerance of Kentucky bluegrass, but thrives in damp shaded areas. Sensitive to pests and diseases. Requires frequent watering. Plant by seed in the fall or spring. (2.2 million seeds/lb. Recommend 2 lbs./1,000 sq. ft. Germinates in 6–30 days. Mow 1 1/2–2 in. high.)

Perennial Ryegrass

Lolium perenne

Frequently used to overseed dormant winter lawns of warm-season grasses (see pgs. 60–61). Grows quickly and remains green throughout cool weather. Glossy green, fine-textured blades. Stands up to heavy foot traffic, drought tolerant. Plant by seed or sod in the fall or spring. (230,000 seeds/lb. Recommend 7 lbs./1,000 sq. ft. Germinates in 3–7 days. Mow 1 1/2–2 in. high.)

CHOOSING GRASS TYPES
COOL-SEASON GRASSES

Chewings Fescue

Festuca rubra commutata

A fast-growing, fine-bladed grass that mixes well with Kentucky bluegrass, especially in cool climates. Grows well in shade and survives with little water. Susceptible to fungal diseases. Easily damaged by foot traffic. Plant by seed in fall or spring. (615,000 seeds/lb. Recommend 5 lbs./1,000 sq. ft. Germinates in 8–14 days. Mow 1–2 1/2 in. high.)

Creeping Red Fescue

Festuca rubra rubra

Like other fescues, tends to clump if grown alone, but mixes well with other cool-season grasses. Fine-textured with dark-green, narrow blades. Grows well in shade and is drought-tolerant, but fares poorly in hot, wet climates. Plant by seed in fall or spring. (615,000 seeds/lb. Recommend 5 lbs./1,000 sq. ft. Germinates in 8–14 days. Mow 1/2–2 1/2 in. high.)

Hard Fescue

Festuca ovina var. *duriuscula* or *longifolia*

Although not as aggressive and quick to establish as creeping and chewings fescue, hard fescue performs better in hot weather, wears better and is more disease resistant. Grows well in shade and requires little water. Plant by seed in fall or spring. (595,000 seeds/lb. Recommend 5 lbs./1,000 sq. ft. Germinates in 8–14 days. Mow 1 1/2–2 1/2 in. high.)

Tall Fescue

Festuca arundinacea

New turf-type tall fescue has a finer blade, improved disease resistance and slower growth than common fescue. Tall fescue has broad, coarse leaves and may be used on playing fields. Although more heat tolerant, it does not mix as well as other fescues. It grows best in areas with mild winters and warm summers. Plant by seed or sod in fall or spring. (230,000 seeds/lb. Recommend 10 lbs./1,000 sq. ft. Germinates in 7–12 days. Mow 1 1/2–2 in. high.)

Annual Ryegrass

Lolium multiflorum

Lives only one year. Coarse bladed and sometimes used for temporary overseeding of dormant, warm-season grasses. Often used to protect slower-germinating varieties. Grows quickly from fall to spring. Poor shade, heat and cold tolerance. Plant by seed in fall or spring. (230,000 seeds/lb. Recommend 7 lbs./1,000 sq. ft. Germinates in 3–7 days. Mow 1 1/2–2 in. high.)

CHOOSING GRASS TYPES
WARM-SEASON GRASSES

Bahiagrass

Paspalum notatum

Brazilian import with an extensive root system that makes it valued for erosion control. Drought tolerant, grows well in sandy and infertile soil and stands up to heavy foot traffic. Has coarse blades, requires frequent mowing and is susceptible to fungal disease. Plant by seed or sod in the spring. (272,000 seeds/lb. Recommend 8 lbs./1,000 sq. ft. Germinates in 21–28 days. Mow 2–3 in. high.)

Common Bermudagrass

Cynodon dactylon

Heat tolerant and durable, its coarse texture, yellow-green color and need for frequent, deep watering makes it inferior to modern hybrids. Plant by seed in the spring. (1,800,000 seeds/lb. Recommend 2–3 lbs./1,000 sq. ft. Germinates in 10–20 days. Mow 3/4–1 1/2 in. high.)

Hybrid Improved Bermudagrass

Cynodon species

More drought tolerant, finer textured and a deeper green than common bermudagrass. Requires less water and is more disease tolerant. Durable, but requires full sun and regular thatch control. Plant by sod or sprigs in spring. (Mow 1/2–1 in. high, using reel mower—grass will turn yellow if allowed to grow higher.)

Centipedegrass

Eremochloa ophiuroides

Medium-textured, light green grass. Best in warm, humid areas. Requires frequent watering. Makes an excellent, low-maintenance lawn. Grows well in infertile and acidic soils. Disease resistant. Highly sensitive to cold temperatures. Shallow-rooted, not good grass for a play lawn. Plant by seed in spring. (875,000 seeds/lb. Recommend 1/4–1/2 lb./1,000 sq. ft. Germinates in 14–20 days. Mow 1–2 in. high.)

Seashore Paspalum

Paspalum vaginatum

Australian import is an alternative to bermudagrass. Thrives in cool coastal regions. Aggressive and durable. Tolerant of drought, heat, pests and salty soils. Browns (goes dormant) quickly in cold weather. Requires slightly more water than bermudagrass. Likes full sun. Plant in the spring with sod. (Mow 3/4–1 in. high.)

CHOOSING GRASS TYPES
WARM-SEASON AND NATIVE GRASSES

St. Augustinegrass

Stenotaphrum secundatum

Tough, broad-bladed grass excellent for play yards. Grows well in both sunny and densely shaded areas. Loves heat. Aggressive and resists weeds. Highly sensitive to chinch bugs and disease. Requires frequent watering and thatch removal. Grows best in warm, coastal areas. Can survive salty soil. (Plant by sod, sprigs or plugs. Mow 1 1/2–2 in. high.)

Zoysiagrass

Zoysia species

Fine-bladed, tough and can survive in the heat without much water. It grows best in warm regions. Resists most insects except billbugs. Grows slowly but once rooted makes a lush and beautiful lawn. Grows in shade, but browns (goes dormant) quickly in winter. (Plant by sod, sprigs or plugs. Mow 1–2 in. high.)

Saltgrass, Fults

Pulccinellia distans

A low growing bunch grass that can reach heights to 16 in., but usually is mowed to medium-fine turf. Dark green leaves with excellent tolerance to salt or alkaline soils. Needs full sun. Plant by sod or seed. (1,940,000 seeds/lb. Recommend 2–3 lb./1000 sq.ft. Germinates in 14 to 21 days. Mow 2 in. high.)

Dichondra

Dichondra micrantha

Bright green groundcover—not a grass, but produces a thick carpet of heart-shaped leaves that give the appearance of a lush lawn. Heat tolerant and surprisingly durable. Requires frequent, thorough watering. Susceptible to pests. Weeds may be difficult to control. Plant in the spring or fall by seed, sod or plugs. (215,000 seeds/lb. Recommend 1/4–1/2 lb./1,000 sq. ft. Germinates in 14–24 days. Mow 3/4–2 in. high.)

Buffalograss

Buchloe dactyloides

Once grew wild across the entire prairie, becoming a popular lawn grass. Requires little water and grows well in heat. May turn brown during the winter. Fine-bladed, it forms a dense, pale green lawn. Only grows to 4 or 5 inches, requires little mowing. Germinates quickly and withstands heavy foot traffic. Plant by seed. (Recommend 1/2–1 1/2 lbs./1000 sq. ft. Germinates in 14–20 days. Mow 1 1/2–2 in. high.)

IDENTIFYING COMMON WEEDS

Annual Bluegrass
Poa annua

Bright, green grass is a stubborn weed in spring and fall. Produces wheat-like seed blossoms that gives lawns a white, mottled look. Often dies out when the weather turns hot.

Bermudagrass
Cynodon dactylon

Bermudagrass becomes a persistent weed when it grows unwanted. Grows aggressively during the summer. Often mistaken for crabgrass, but its blades are finer and smaller.

Dallisgrass
Paspalum dilatatum

One of the most common summer weeds. Long, coarse-bladed leaves grow ring-like pattern close to the ground. It grows best in wet areas.

LAWN WEEDS

Weeds are plants that grow where they aren't wanted. Even in carefully tended lawns, some weeds are sure to grow. Weed seeds blow in with the wind or are carried in by people, animals and water. Some weed seeds may be included in packages of grass seed. Label laws require that the percentage of weed seeds be stated on all turf grass packages.

There are two types of weeds: narrowleaf and broadleaf. Narrowleaf weeds are grasses other than the ones you want in your lawn. Bermudagrass, annual bluegrass, dallisgrass quackgrass and crabgrass are the primary culprits. They compete strongly and can drive out other, less hardy grasses if allowed to grow unchecked. Crabgrass is probably the most prevalent, growing in most areas. It spreads vertically to form 2–4 in. flat clumps with long, spindly leaves and seed stems.

Crabgrass is a pest during spring and summer. It grows quickly in warm and hot weather and may invade your lawn when cool-season grasses go dormant during summer. Annual bluegrass and other cool-season grasses are most visible during the spring and fall, when they grow quickly.

Broadleafed weeds include all non-grassy weeds and are usually easy to spot. Their wide leaves stand out against the narrow grasses. Some of the most common broad-leafed weeds are dandelions, plantain, chickweed and spotted spurge.

Most weeds can be controlled through good lawn practices such as proper mowing, watering, dethatching and fertilizing. Chemical controls can also be used to prevent them from sprouting or to kill them after they appear (see pg. 42).

Dandelion

Taraxacum officinale

Most recognizable of weeds. Bright yellow flower and round, white seed-head are unmistakable. Grow from a single taproot. May regrow if broken off.

IDENTIFYING COMMON WEEDS

Oxalis
Oxalis corniculata

Looks like clover, grows like dandelion. Small, clover-like leaves are green or purple and grow from a shallow tap root. In spring pods explode like popcorn to toss seeds nearly 6 ft.

Curly Dock
Rumex crispus

Broadleafed, with narrow, curled and scalloped leaves sometimes mistaken for a dandelion. Spreads horizontally and, if not killed, sends up a thin stalk of greenish flowers. Grows spring and fall.

Mallow or Cheeseweed
Malva species

Small, round leaves give it a delicate look, but it is really as tough as crabgrass. Light green, fan-shaped leaves on top of thin, whitish stalks. Appears first in spring, but grows through summer and fall. Grows taller than grass.

Knotweed
Polygonum aviculare

Spindly, almond-shaped leaves grow sparsely along a vertical stalk. Grows in bunches that appear as one large, thick plant. Leaves are pale green and easy to identify. Grows spring and fall.

Plantain

Plantago species

This cool-season weed grows in spring and fall. Oval-shaped leaves form rosettes up to 6 in. across. Slender flower stalk curls at the top, makes it easy to identify.

Quackgrass

Agropyron repens

Thick, long blades like dallisgrass, but it doesn't grow in distinctive ring. Leaves grow quickly and can reach 3 ft. if unmowed. Flowering spikes look like tiny heads of wheat. Grows spring and fall.

Spotted Spurge

Euphorbia maculata

Looks like clover but small green leaves have a small red spot near the center and grow from white or red stalks. Grows low to the ground. Appears in spring and grows until fall.

RESTORING LAWNS

Some lawns have grown for more than 100 years. Even so, all lawns require special care from time to time. This includes replanting entire sections that have gone bare or become overrun with weeds. Lawn restoration isn't difficult and it will renew your lawn's lush, green beauty.

First Remove all grass and weeds. Withhold water to the area and cover it with black plastic, or use a chemical herbicide containing *glyphosate* to kill all plants growing in the area to be restored.

Then Rake and remove dead weeds or use a sod cutter, available for rent at lawn centers.

Third Test soil and measure area. Add necessary amendments and fertilizers and mix completely into the soil.

Fourth Carefully level lawn area so water won't puddle or run off. Apply seed.

Next Rake lightly, then roll to smooth the surface and press the seeds into the soil.

Last Sprinkle thin layer of peat moss atop seeds and roll. Keep moist until seeds germinate, using fine spray.

Amendments and Fertilizers

An important step in restoring lawns is adding soil amendments and fertilizers. Amendments are either organic or inorganic.

Organic amendments come from plant and animal material and help your soil absorb and retain water. They also release nutrients into the soil that are vital to growing turf. Organic amendments include composted manure, wood shavings, ground bark, peat moss, sawdust and many kinds of plant by-products, such as ground-up hay.

Some organic amendments, such as raw wood chips and shavings, can rob your soil of nitrogen as they decompose. Be sure to add 1 lb. of ammonium sulfate for every 1 in. deep layer of wood-fiber amendment you apply. Place a 2–4 in. layer of amendment on the lawn surface you are restoring, then mix it in thoroughly.

Find your soil's nutrient content by having a professional laboratory test your soil or by taking soil samples to your agricultural extension office. These tests are usually more accurate than home test kits, if somewhat more expensive.

Inorganic amendments usually do not contain nutrients, but are very useful in helping to aerify and drain your soil. They include lime and gypsum, which also help balance too-acidic soils.

Also check your soil for compaction. Plunge a long screwdriver into the turf at several spots. If it is difficult to push in, use an aerifier (see pgs. 38–39).

Finally, either add a balanced fertilizer or one that provides the balance of nutrients recommended in your soil test.

ALTERNATIVES TO SEEDING LAWNS

First Pick a grass type suited to your climate available either as sod, sprigs or plugs. It should be moist, not dry and cracked or sopping wet.

Then Measure the number of square feet in your lawn, adding about 10% allowance when you order your sod, sprigs or plugs. Use the installation method shown.

Sodding

Third Aerify the soil, then add amendments and fertilizers.

Fourth Fit strips tightly, avoiding gaps. Cut with a sharp knife around any obstacles.

Last Press sod into soil bed with half-filled water roller. Make 3 separate passes.

Sprigging

Third Aerify the soil, then add amendments and fertilizers.

Either Scatter sprigs atop seed bed. Cover lightly with peat. Roll with cleated roller.

Or Plant sprigs 6–8 in. apart. Cover lightly with peat. Roll with cleated roller.

Plugging

Third Cut checkerboard pattern of holes with plugging tool.

Fourth Sprinkle balanced fertilizer in each hole.

Next Set each plug in hole, then press firmly.

Last Keep constantly moist with a fine spray of water. Water daily for the first 4–6 weeks until rooted.

ALTERNATIVES TO SEEDING

There are a number of alternatives to planting your lawn by seed. Sod, sprigs and plugs are popular methods.

Sod allows you to have lush green grass within hours. With proper watering, the root system will be fully established within two weeks. Sod comes in rolled strips, usually 6–9 ft. long and 18 in. across. You install it much the same way you lay down a carpet inside your house. The sod strips can be cut easily with a knife so you can fit the sod snugly around sprinklers, sidewalks, fences, flower beds and other borders.

Use care when you purchase sod strips—don't buy them if the grass is yellowing or the turf has large cracks in it. Those are signs that it hasn't been watered correctly. Sod can be laid at nearly any time of the year except during freezing weather. Most grasses are available in sod strips. Sod may be more expensive than seeding or other lawn installation methods.

Many warm-season grasses, such as bermudagrass, carpetgrass, centipede-grass, St. Augustinegrass and zoysia, can also be planted using sprigs. Sprigs—also called stolons or runners—contain both leaves and roots. They can be purchased already separated, or you can buy sod and cut out the sprigs yourself. Be sure to keep them moist until planting. As soon as possible after purchase, plant them in furrowed rows, from 6–12 in. apart. You can also press them into the soil 6–8 in. apart around your yard.

Warm-season grasses can be planted as plugs—small squares or circles of grass and soil that have been cut from sod. These are planted in intervals around the lawn, then kept moist.

The best time to plant sprigs and plugs is in the spring or early fall.

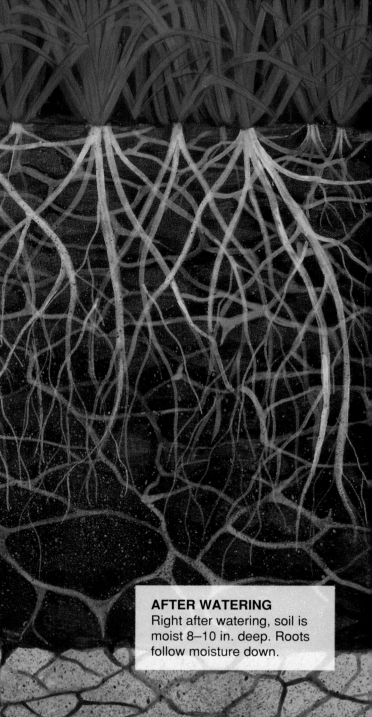

WATERING LAWNS

Water your lawn with 1 in. of water, applied all at once (or in several smaller doses if water starts to run off). Water again when top 2 inches of soil dries. To test, plunge a screwdriver into the turf. If it goes in too easily, wait a day or two and check again.

CORRECT WATERING

It's important that all your lawn receives equal amounts of water. Check it by placing equal-sized containers in a grid pattern around your lawn. Start a timer, then turn on your watering system. After 15 minutes, check the water depth in each container. Each should be equal. If there's more than a 1/4-in. difference between the containers, adjust or change your sprinklers. Test again and keep adjusting with each watering until the system waters your lawn evenly. Use the amount collected in 15 minutes to tell how long to water to apply 1 in. of total water.

The slope and grade of your lawn is also important. Water will run off a lawn that is sloped too much. One that is uneven will puddle with wet and dry areas.

Soil probes that measure soil moisture can help you determine how much moisture is reaching the roots of your grass. Most lawn centers have several models for every price range and desired feature.

AFTER WATERING
Right after watering, soil is moist 8–10 in. deep. Roots follow moisture down.

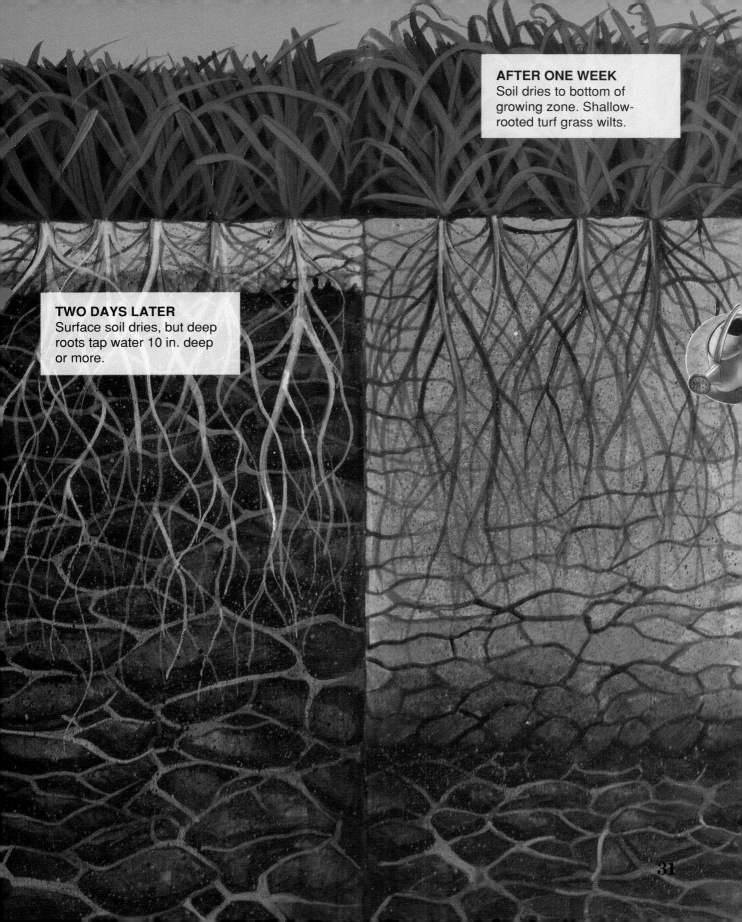

AFTER ONE WEEK
Soil dries to bottom of growing zone. Shallow-rooted turf grass wilts.

TWO DAYS LATER
Surface soil dries, but deep roots tap water 10 in. deep or more.

31

Underground Lawn Sprinkler System

Planning Sprinklers

Underground, automatic sprinkler systems are easy and efficient. Installation isn't hard, but will usually take several weekends.

Basic parts include an automatic timer, control valves, pipes and pipe fittings, sprinkler heads, risers, anti-siphon valves and drain-out valves, necessary if your area freezes in winter.

First test your water pressure, then map your system as a scale drawing. Workbooks are available along with free advice at many lawn centers. Plot lines and sprinklers along the perimeter of your lawn, with quarter-circle sprinkler heads in the corners, half-circle heads along the edges and, if needed, full-circle heads in the middle. Overlap every head's spray pattern for even coverage. Make a separate "circuit" for each area or group of sprinklers.

Once you've planned the type and number of sprinklers, purchase pipe and all components. Dig trenches 12–16 in. deep, either by hand or with a trenching machine. Cut pipe sections to length and lay out the whole system in the trenches with loose joints before applying any glue. When everything fits correctly, join them together with primer and glue.

Next, install sprinkler risers of the correct height. Then build the manifold and tap into the main service line, as described on the opposite page. Before attaching the sprinkler heads, flush the system of dirt and debris by running water through it.

In areas with freezing temperatures, be sure to install a self-draining valve at the lowest part of the system.

First Water line pressure must be at least 20 psi. Use a pressure gauge, available at lawn centers and plumbing supply stores.

Then Draw system, using graph paper. No circuit should exceed the gallons per minute available at the main service.

Third List and buy all materials, consulting with your lawn center specialist.

CAUTION

Check that local codes allow use of PVC pipe.

Fourth Remove and save turf. Dig V-shaped trenches by hand or use a trenching machine.

Next Assemble, glue and attach to water supply. Flush to clear any debris before installing sprinkler heads.

Last Check coverage, adjust and backfill trenches. Return removed sod and water.

MANIFOLD AND CONNECTION

Each sprinkler circuit has its own control valve, operated manually or electrically by an automatic timer. They all should be placed together in a "manifold," with each connected to its circuit on one side and to the main water supply line on the other.

An anti-siphon valve on every circuit stops sprinkler water from draining into your home's drinking water.

To tap into the supply line, turn off the house's water at the meter. Cut the supply pipe, and install a compression tee and shutoff valve. Follow all applicable building codes for your area. If you have a water softener, always install sprinklers between the softener and the meter. Then attach the tee to the sprinkler supply line and manifold. Use the same method to tap into basement or existing outside faucet lines.

HOSES AND SPRINKLERS

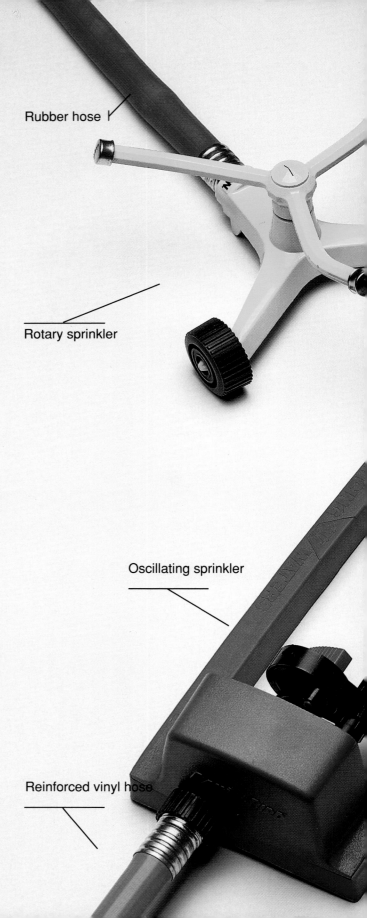

Rubber hose

Rotary sprinkler

Oscillating sprinkler

Reinforced vinyl hose

WATERING EQUIPMENT

Hose-end sprinklers come in a variety of shapes, each with its own spray pattern. Most versatile is the impulse sprinkler. It covers a wide area with a strong jet of water, then reverses itself to cover a smaller area with a fine spray.

Pressure-driven oscillating sprinklers shoot a fan-shaped spray of water while moving slowly back and forth. They water gently and are excellent for new lawns or for spot-watering.

Revolving-arm sprinklers have multiple heads that whirl in a circle, covering the lawn with a fine spray. Easy to move, they are often mounted on wheels.

Cone sprinklers cover small areas with a fountain-like pattern.

Choose from four basic types of hoses: rubber, vinyl, reinforced rubber and vinyl and reinforced vinyl.

Rubber hoses are flexible and durable, but heavy compared with the other types. They are a dull green color.

Vinyl hoses are shiny and lightweight. They are inexpensive, but not so durable.

Reinforced rubber and vinyl hoses contain tough fiber cord. They are sturdy, flexible and rarely suffer kinks. Their outsides are shiny, with a textured look.
Reinforced vinyl hoses are more durable than plain vinyl. Cold weather damages them.

Hoses usually come in three sizes (measured by their inside diameter): 1/2 in. for small lawns and shrubs, 5/8 in. for medium-sized lawns and gardens and 3/4 in. for large lawns. Common lawn sprinklers will fit all of these hoses, regardless of the hose size.

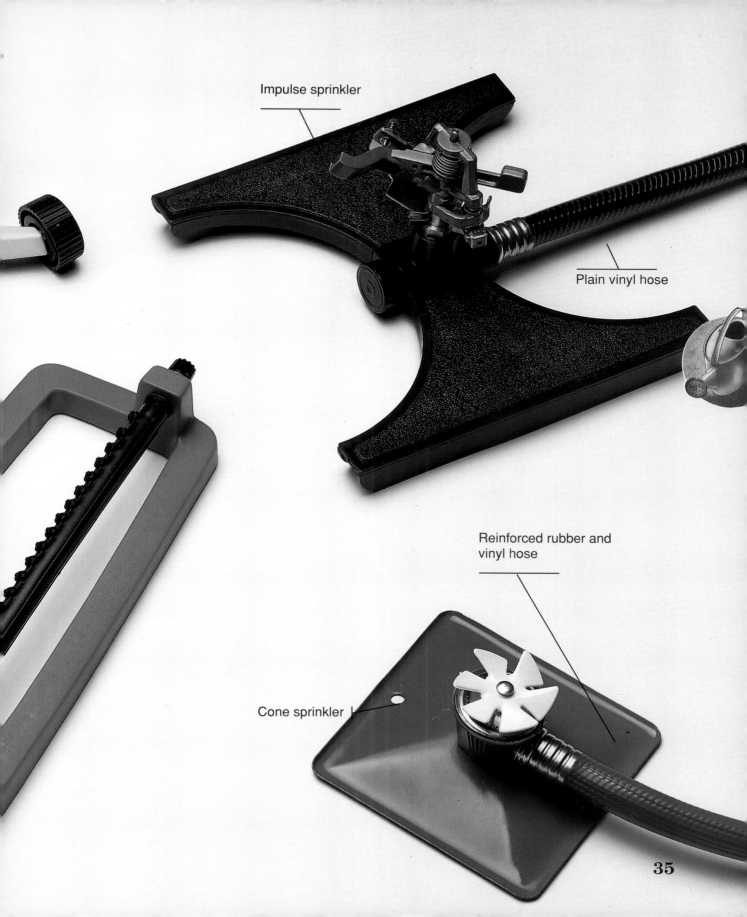

Impulse sprinkler

Plain vinyl hose

Reinforced rubber and
vinyl hose

Cone sprinkler

35

MOWING LAWNS

MOWING NEW LAWNS

Newly planted grass takes a few weeks to become established, and care should be taken during first mowings to avoid damaging it. Reel mowers work best because they are gentle and cut cleanly. Cut after the grass has dried from the morning dew. Turn corners carefully to avoid uprooting tender grass with the wheels.

Don't be afraid to mow your new lawn, though. Mowing will encourage the grass to grow and help it spread. A good general rule is to leave the clippings in the lawn—they make an ideal fertilizer.

Mow the grass when it grows one-third taller than its recommended height (see pgs. 14–21). For example, if the ideal height of your grass is 2 in., then mow it when the blades first reach 3 in. high. Adjust your sharpened mower to cut 2 in. high, but no lower. Scalping young grass usually kills it. It is very important that your mower be sharp; dull blades pull and rip, sometimes pulling out clumps of young grass.

Soil should be firm and dry when you mow. Withhold water the day before so mower wheels won't create ruts. During wet periods hold off mowing until the soil dries out a little. Newly cut grass will grow best if it is watered immediately after it is mowed.

WHEN TO CUT

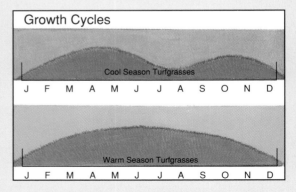

Mow your grass when it is one-third taller than its recommended height. How often to mow depends on the type of grass, how much you fertilize and water it and the season. Grass doesn't grow at the same rate all year round. For example, bluegrass may need cutting twice a week in spring and fall but only every other week during the summer. Frequent watering and fertilizing promotes vigorous growth and frequent mowings.

Don't cut on a time schedule. Instead, match your mowing times to the lawn's growth rate. Cutting the right height when needed encourages healthy growth, makes it look beautiful and allows it to resist diseases and pests. This, in turn, reduces the need for care or pesticides.

Always cut to the right height. Leaving it too high will cause long and stringy growth and a coarse look. Cutting too short—scalping—causes severe damage by shocking and sometimes killing the roots.

Grasses differ in their optimum mowing heights because they grow differently. Cool-season grasses grow vertically, but warm-season grasses grow more horizontally in a thicker mat. All grasses need an optimum amount of leaf surface to stay healthy, and cool-season grasses are cut higher to have the leaf surface they need. Warm-season grasses need to be lower to prompt growth.

Mowing

Lawn mowers are either rotary or reel type. Rotary mower blades spin horizontally. They are most popular because of their low cost, durability and flexibility. Reel mowers have blades that rotate in a circle above the turf. They cut grass cleanly and are used on the best lawns and golf courses.

The power rotary mower is most popular. Powered either by electricity or gas, it cuts while going backward and forward and is tough enough to handle rough terrain.

A variation is the self-propelled rotary mower. Unlike their hand-pushed cousins, they travel forward under their own power. Steering is simple, and the price is nearly the same as for standard power mowers. For homes with large lawns or for those who prefer not to use mowing the lawn as a workout, they may be a good answer.

Another common rotary mower is the ride-on mower or mini-tractor. They are ideal for large lawns.

Motorized reel mowers are expensive, but highly efficient. They are often used on large, finely manicured lawns and on golf course putting greens, tees and fairways.

Hand-pushed, non-motorized reel mowers are quieter, lighter and less expensive than any power mowers. They are easy to handle. Use them to mow small lawns.

Trimming and Edging

Trimming and edging gives your lawn a finished look. Mowers usually leave some tall grass in the corners of the lawn, against wall, fences or trees. You'll need a special tool to cut it. Hand shears or clippers will do small jobs, but if you need something larger, try a motorized trimmer.

Most popular is the hand-held string trimmer, which whips down weeds and grass with a spinning nylon string. Electric types are light, easy to use and better for small trimming jobs. Always use string trimmers carefully around trees or shrubs to avoid damaging their bark and growth tissues.

Another type of trimmer uses metal blades to bite into grass. It is gas-powered and is more precise than string trimmers.

Edgers give a manicured look to your lawn by creating carefully cut edges around sidewalks, lawn borders and flower beds. Small, inexpensive, manually operated edgers may be all that's needed.

There are also a number of motorized edgers from which to choose, including electric (some are cordless) and gas-powered types. Pick from long-handled or short-handled models.

Always wear protective eyewear and use caution when operating a trimmer or edger.

DETHATCHING AND AERIFICATION

THATCH BUILDUP

Sooner or later most lawns suffer from too much thatch. Thatch is a brownish layer of dead leaves, stems, roots and other debris that builds up between the soil and the grass blades. Some thatch is actually good for the grass. It protects the roots and helps keep the soil from compacting. But when thatch builds up over 1/2 in. thick, it begins to hold water and blocks it from the roots. It may even cause the lawn to die of thirst. A thick thatch layer can deprive the roots of nutrients and provide a perfect home for pests and diseases.

Some grasses accumulate thatch quickly, including warm-season grasses such as bermudagrass, St. Augustinegrass and zoysia and cool-season grasses such as bentgrass and Kentucky bluegrass.

Most grasses should be dethatched at least once a year. Some, including those just listed, may need even more frequent treatment. To check the thatch depth in your own lawn, cut out a small section of turf. If the thatch layer is much more than 1/2 in., it's time to thin it. Another symptom of too much thatch is when your mower begins to scalp the grass in unusual patterns. That happens when the mower wheels sink into the thatch layer.

Cool-season grasses should be dethatched in the fall and warm-season grasses in the early spring.

It's a good idea to aerate your lawn at the same time that you dethatch it. Aeration consists of cutting holes in your lawn with a special machine. It helps clear out the thatch and reduces soil compaction. This allows moisture, oxygen and nutrients to move more freely to the roots.

Dethatching

First Measure the thatch layer with a ruler. Thin it when it becomes thicker than 1/2 in.

Next Dethatching machines or vertical mowers slice through the thatch layer with knife-like blades.

Last Set the blades to penetrate the thatch layer and the top 1/4 in. of soil. Rake thoroughly.

Aerification

First Compacted soil kills grass by blocking nutrients, air and water to grass roots.

Next Aerification machines penetrate 2–3 in. and remove cores or plugs. Make two passes over your lawn.

Last Apply water to soil cores to wash them into the lawn. Grass roots quickly fill in holes.

CAUTION

Wear safety glasses and shoes when using power lawn equipment.

CHOOSING FERTILIZERS

Most fertilizers are labeled with three numbers, such as 15-10-5. Each number tells the percentage by weight of nitrogen, phosphorus and potassium. A complete, balanced fertilizer—best for new lawns—contains nearly equal amounts of each nutrient.

Your lawn or garden store can make recommendations, or soil tests help find the best ratio for your lawn (see pgs. 26-27).

Fertilizers are either organic or synthetic. Organic fertilizers are made from the remains of plants and animals, such as blood, bone, hoof, fish and horn meal, manures and plant meal. They release nutrients slowly, but are not balanced. They may not always release their nutrients during the growing season of your turfgrasses.

Synthetic fertilizers are manufactured from inorganic minerals and chemicals. They are made to release their nutrients quickly, giving immediate results (a lush green lawn), but the results are not long-lasting.

Both types come in dry and liquid forms. Dry fertilizers dissolve with each watering and may release nutrients for two or three months. Liquids are applied with a hose-end sprayer and start to work immediately, but they don't last long and are generally more expensive.

Applying Lawn Fertilizer

First Check the fertilizer label and determine the correct rate to apply.

Then Set a drop or broadcast spreader to 1/2 the label recommended rate.

Third Apply fertilizer in parallel rows, overlapping your wheel tracks.

Last Apply a second pass at right angles to the first to complete the job.

WHEN AND HOW TO APPLY

Fertilize most grasses during their growing seasons, usually spring and fall. Most fertilizers come with instructions on their label that indicate their use and best time for application.

Apply fertilizer by one of three methods: broadcast spreading, drop spreading or liquid spraying—hand-casting is not recommended.

Broadcast spread with a hand-operated or a walk-behind applicator to throw dry fertilizer from a hopper onto the lawn. Broadcast spreading is fast and efficient. Be sure to apply in criss-cross strips as shown for full coverage.

Drop spreading is the recommended way to apply dry fertilizer. The walk-behind spreader drops an even amount of fertilizer across the lawn but takes longer than the other methods. Drop spreaders can be purchased or rented from lawn centers. Adjust the outlet flow, following fertilizer or spreader label instructions, or ask for advice from your lawn center.

Visually check that you applied the fertilizer evenly. Always overlap wheel tracks to avoid missing areas. Uneven fertilization causes ragged growth and may burn your lawn. If necessary, spread it further with a garden rake, and always water the fertilizer in right after you finish applying it.

Liquid fertilizers are easily applied by using a garden hose-end sprayer. The fertilizer container will tell you the fertilizer-to-water mix. Before you begin spraying, try to get an idea of the midpoint of your lawn. By the time you reach it, you should have used about half of the liquid fertilizer in the hose container. Even liquid fertilizers can burn a lawn if applied in too strong a concentration.

WEED CONTROL
PROBLEMS AND CURES

Grassy Weeds

Some grassy weeds may yield to pre-emergent controls, but most must be hand pulled or killed with a broad-spectrum herbicide containing glyphosate.

Annual bluegrass
Bentgrass
Bermudagrass
Quackgrass
Crabgrass
Goosegrass
Dallisgrass
Tall fescue
Barnyardgrass
Nutsedge
Velvetgrass

Broadleafed Weeds

Use a post-emergent herbicide labeled to control broadleafed weeds, or pull by hand.

Wild garlic
Prostrate knotweed
Clover
Oxalis
Mouse-ear chickweed
Spotted spurge
Common chickweed
Henbit
English lawn daisy
Purslane
Ground ivy
Curly dock
Dandelion
Sheep sorrel
Mallow
Buckhorn and broadleaf plantain
Morning glory

Other Weeds

Moss
  Treat with copper sulfate as directed in label instructions.

Algae
  Treat with maneb, mancozeb. Apply twice, 1 mo. apart in early spring.

Mushrooms
  Improve lawn drainage and fertilize. Remove by hand or lawn mower.

Winter-killed grasses
  In warm-season grass lawns, eliminate dead annual bluegrass, crabgrass and dormant bermudagrass by hand and overseed with winter grasses such as perennial ryegrass.

PREVENTING WEEDS

The best weed control method is prevention through good lawn maintenance. Proper mowing, fertilizing, watering, dethatching and aerification will usually keep weeds to a minimum. Occasionally, though, weeds will grow in your lawn and be unsightly.

Weeds come in two types: grassy or broadleafed. Grassy weeds (see pgs. 22–25) are simply grasses other than the type you want growing in your lawn. They may strengthen your lawn by adding diversity, but are a nuisance if you don't want them there. In transition climates warm-season grasses such as bermudagrass may invade your lawn during the summer, while cool-season grasses such as annual bluegrass may appear in spring and fall.

Broadleafed weeds are all the other, non-grassy weeds (see pgs. 22–25). They are easier to identify and eliminate than grassy weeds and are usually easy to pull by hand.

Moss, algae and mushrooms are special types of "weeds" that usually result from poor drainage, too much watering or lack of fertilizer. Like grassy and broadleafed weeds, these can either be hand pulled or raked out of the yard, or chemical controls will eliminate them.

If your weeds have become a major problem, you may wish to use chemical controls. There are two basic types: pre-emergent and post-emergent herbicides. Pre-emergent controls are applied before weed seeds begin to germinate and weed plants grow. Post-emergent controls are applied after the weed is growing and has been identified. Many common weeds are named in the accompanying lists of grassy, broadleaf and other weeds.

Weed Control
Pre-emergent Control

Herbicides can be applied in a number of ways. The most common is the hose-end sprayer, but pressure-spray tanks and pump sprayers are also used. Pressure-spray tanks are useful because they allow you to spot-treat areas by hand. Like all pesticides, herbicides should be applied only as directed on the label.

PREVENTING WEED GROWTH

If you are familiar with the type of weeds that are likely to infest your lawn, you can use herbicides to destroy many of them before they have a chance to grow.

Destroying sprouting weeds as they reach the soil surface is called pre-emergent control. Apply the pre-emergent herbicides depending upon your climate and the type of weeds you are trying to eliminate because different weeds germinate in different seasons—your lawn or garden store will advise you.

Like all herbicides, pre-emergent herbicides can kill or injure your lawn, and they contain artificial or naturally occurring poisons that are released into the environment. It is important to use weed killers only as directed.

Every herbicide label contains specific directions, a list of the weeds for which it is effective, the active chemical ingredients and whether it is harmful to turf grasses. It also lists other important information about the herbicide. Always read the entire label and completely follow all directions when applying weed killers.

In general, apply all herbicides on calm days without wind. Never reuse containers used for mixing chemicals, and dispose of them as directed on the label. Ask your lawn expert or county Agricultural Extension Service about how long the active ingredients in each herbicide remain potent. Avoid allowing children or animals to use the lawn until it is safe.

Some herbicidal chemicals—such as dicamba and 2,4-D—are restricted and require a permit for use from local regulatory agencies. Information may be obtained at your garden store or nursery.

GROWING WEEDS

Eliminating weeds after seeds germinate and grow is called post-emergent control. There are several control methods.

Control weeds with good lawn care. Most grasses will compete successfully against weeds if the lawn is properly mowed, watered and fertilized. However, even well-maintained lawns are sometimes plagued with weeds.

Pulling or digging weeds out by hand or with a weed remover is usually quick and effective. Its benefits include removing only the weeds and reducing herbicide exposure to the turf and yourself.

Larger areas may require chemicals—choose either selective or non-selective. Selective herbicides kill only certain plant types—broadleafed weeds, for example—but will not harm lawn grasses. They are ideal for many different weeds. Non-selective herbicides—such as *glyphosate*—kill all treated plants. Some are short-lived and allow reseeding of the area less than a week after application, while others sterilize the soil.

As with other chemical controls, always read and follow the directions on the herbicide label completely before applying the herbicide to your lawn.

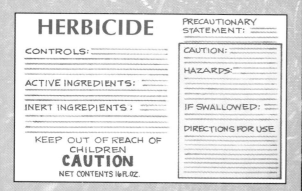

HERBICIDE

PRECAUTIONARY STATEMENT:

CONTROLS:

ACTIVE INGREDIENTS:

INERT INGREDIENTS:

CAUTION:

HAZARDS:

IF SWALLOWED:

DIRECTIONS FOR USE

KEEP OUT OF REACH OF CHILDREN
CAUTION
NET CONTENTS 16 FL. OZ.

Hand apply non-selective herbicides carefully to avoid damage to desirable plants and turfgrasses.

Use hose-end sprayers when applying selective herbicides. Take care to spray desired areas only.

Carefully remove plant and entire root when hand-pulling weeds to prevent regrowth. Weeding tools make the job easier.

INSECT, LARVAE AND GRUB PESTS

Armyworms

Pseudaletia unipuncta

Whitish moths with yellow front wings lay eggs for 1-in., white-and-brown-striped larvae. Control: diazinon, chlorpyrifos or carbaryl.

Billbugs

Sphenophorus species

Both brown and black weevil adult with long snout and white, legless grub feed on grass roots. Control: diazinon or carbaryl.

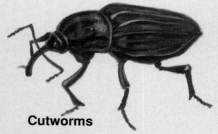

Cutworms

Pseudaletia species

Brown/black, 1/4 in., flying insects leave yellow spots. Push bottomless can into turf at edge of yellow patch, fill with water. Bugs will float to top. Control: diazinon and chlorpyrifos.

Chinch bugs

Blissus species

Common, larvae are 1–2-in. whitish grubs with black spots or stripes on sides. They leave ragged, brown patches. Mix 1 tbsp. household detergent in 1 gal. water and pour onto 1 sq. yd. of lawn. Larvae rise to surface. Control: diazinon or chlorpyrifos.

Leafhoppers

Cicadellidae family

Tiny green grasshoppers that fly up in bunches leave lawns dry and yellow-green. Control: diazinon or acephate.

Mole crickets

Scapteriscus species

Large 2-in. larvae tunnel through turf, eating and destroying grass roots. Control: bait containing propoxur.

Sod webworms

Crambus sperryellus

Gray caterpillars spin silken tunnels through thatch, become beige-colored moths. Leave ragged brown patches. Detect same as cutworms. Control: diazinon, chlorpyrifos or carbaryl.

White grubs

Cyclocephala species

1–1 1/2-in. larvae of many different beetles have three pairs of legs, destroy roots. Infested grass rolls back like sod. Control: diazinon and chlorpyrifos. Water well.

Bermudagrass mite

Aceria neocynodonis

Shake tiny, yellowish pests from clump of bermudagrass onto dark paper. Control: thatch removal, diazinon.

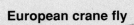

European crane fly

Tipula paludosa

Huge, mosquito-like adults are harmless, but thin, whitish grubs with distinctive ring sections eat leaves and stems. Control: diazinon.

Flea beetles

Chaetocnema repens

Black, flea-like beetles attack dichondra. Control: diazinon or chlorhair pyrifos.

Greenbugs

Schiaphis graminum

Tiny, green aphids suck grass juices. Turf dies in patches. Control: acephate.

Nematodes

Microscopic worms infect roots, killing plants. Control: laboratory analysis is required to confirm nematodes, recommend control.

Ants

Ants don't damage grass but hills are unsightly. Control: Rake out, then apply diazinon or Orthene.

LAWN PESTS

Harmful lawn pests come in three groups: those that live above ground and drink grass fluids; those that live on the soil surface and feed on the leaves and crowns; and those that live underground and eat grass roots.

While pests can damage your lawn, remember that many harmless or helpful insects also live there. Don't kill all of them. Most of the time the harmful ones can be kept to a minimum if you water, mow, fertilize, dethatch and aerify your lawn regularly.

The first step in controlling any pest infestation is to mow the lawn to the correct height, removing all clippings and watering heavily. Use only pesticides specifically named for the pest you have identified. Always follow label instructions for any chemical controls.

Piercing insects that suck plant fluids include chinch bugs, leafhoppers, spider mites and other similar insects. Unchecked, they leave large, dry and yellow patches in your lawn. The insects are usually found on the edges, where the grass is just beginning to yellow. Apply an appropriate control.

Most chewing and boring pests are moth larvae, which appear as worm-like grubs on the grass surface. They include cutworms, sod webworms, fiery skippers and armyworms. Adult moths don't feed on grass, just their larvae. Wait until the grass dries and apply an appropriate control. Wait 48 hours before watering again, then fertilize.

Underground pests include white grubs, ground pearls and other root-eating insects. If yellow or dying grass pulls up easily, suspect these root pests. Check by lifting the sod after cutting with a sharp knife. If many grubs are found, apply a chemical control. Water heavily afterwards, so the insecticide will penetrate the soil.

INSECT PEST CONTROL

CONTROLLING INSECTS

Like herbicides, pesticides are the last resort for pest control.

Prevent harmful insects from infesting and damaging your lawn with proper maintenance and care. Use biological and nontoxic controls instead of insecticides. They reduce harmful insects while allowing their natural enemies to survive.

If insecticides are used after care and non-toxic methods have failed, closely follow all label directions. Never use more than directed—it damages your lawn and the environment.

All pesticide labels carry the chemical names of their active ingredients, the insects killed and directions for timing and application. Choose only insecticides listed for your pest problem. If you have questions, ask your lawn center expert.

Apply insecticides as directed. Most popular is by using a hose-end sprayer that mixes pesticide with water from the hose as it is sprayed onto the lawn. Hand sprayers are used for small areas. Or, apply insecticides with pressure spray tanks or watering cans. Never use a container that held insecticides for any other purpose, and dispose of pesticide-contaminated containers and equipment as directed on the label.

Piercing Insects
Control insects that pierce grass plants and suck out their juices by mowing and removing clippings, then watering heavily. When the grass is dry, apply the recommended insecticide. Do not water again for 2 days.

PEST SPRAY

CONTROLS:

ACTIVE INGREDIENTS:

INERT INGREDIENTS:

KEEP OUT OF REACH OF CHILDREN
CAUTION
NET CONTENTS 16 FL. OZ.

PRECAUTIONARY STATEMENT:

CAUTION:

HAZARDS:

IF SWALLOWED:

DIRECTIONS FOR USE

Soil Insects
These underground pests are difficult to kill using insecticides, especially in lawns with a thick thatch layer. Control them by mowing, dethatching and removing clippings, then apply the appropriate insecticide. Water lightly immediately to help the insecticide penetrate.

Chewing Insects
Gray or brownish moths seen flying around lawns usually are a sign that their larvae—grub-like insects— are present in the lawn. Control them by mowing and removing clippings, then watering heavily. After grass dries, apply an appropriate insecticide. Water again in 2 days, then fertilize.

51

CONTROLLING
NON-INSECT PESTS

DOGS
Urine salts cause round dead spots in healthy lawns. Keep dogs off lawn. Restore by soaking with water, reseeding and fertilizing.

SLUGS AND SNAILS
Live in moist groundcovers, leave silvery trails, eat grass. Control with metaldehyde or methiocarb baits.

MOLES
Tunnels destroy roots and leave dead grass. Moles eat grubs and insects. Treat lawn to get rid of their food supply.

POCKET GOPHERS
Damage lawn by eating roots and plants. Dig into main tunnel. Set traps at each side. Plug with fresh grass, cover with black plastic. Check daily.

BIRDS
Tear lawn surface while searching for insects. Control insects so birds won't be a problem.

EARTHWORMS
Beneficial to lawn. They feed on thatch and aerify soil. Castings should be watered or raked into turf.

GROUND SQUIRRELS
Dwelling holes are unsightly but cause minimal turf damage. Trap like gophers or ignore.

COMMON PROBLEMS

If you've treated the turf for insects, weeds and diseases, and stubborn brown spots still persist, it is time to look at other possible causes, including environmental conditions and non–pest-related problems.

Nematodes, tiny parasites that are abundant in all soils, can sometimes be a problem. Since nematodes are too small to be seen with the naked eye, you must have your soil tested in a professional laboratory. Check with your Agricultural Extension Service to see if nematodes are a problem in your area. If your lawn is infested with harmful nematodes, the laboratory expert can suggest ways to eliminate them.

The most common non-pest lawn problems, though, stem from environmental conditions, such as compacted soil, too much thatch in the grass, depressions in the lawn and shaded areas.

Grass has a tough time growing in hardpan and where there is deep thatch, so aerify and dethatch your lawn regularly (see pgs. 38–39). Watering and fertilizing your lawn too much or too little can also cause it to yellow and grow poorly. If one area continues to struggle while the rest of the lawn looks good, check to see if the area sits too high or too low in the lawn. If it is too high, water will drain off too fast. If it is too low, it will be too wet. Use a shovel to smooth out the area, then reseed.

Trees can also cause persistent yellowing in the lawn by blocking sunlight and rain. Thinning the tree may be necessary to solve the problem.

Sometimes circles of dead grass in your lawn may be caused by dogs. Keep dogs off your lawn and restore the dead areas by soaking them thoroughly, then reseeding.

DISEASE AND FUNGUS

FUNGUS DISEASES

Lawn diseases are caused by various types of fungi. Their attack may turn your lawn brown in a few days. Often, diseases are encouraged by poor lawn care and maintenance. Control thatch and water and fertilize properly to avoid turning your lawn into a haven for disease.

Since diseases thrive in moist thatch layers, regular thatch control and proper watering keep them to a minimum. Water thoroughly, then allow the top 2 in. of soil to dry out before watering again. It is also important that the grass be fertilized regularly, because a lack of nitrogen in the soil can weaken the grass and make it vulnerable to attack from disease. Avoid over-fertilizing.

If diseases persist, dozens of different types of fungicides are available. The fungicides are either systemic or nonsystemic. Systemic fungicides destroy the fungi from the inside of the organism, making them more effective than nonsystemic fungicides, which attack the diseases from the outside. You have to carefully match the fungicide to the disease that is attacking your lawn, though, because they are specific, that is, each kills only certain types of fungal diseases.

Nonsystemic fungicides are more effective when applied about 2 weeks before the disease appears. Of course, that requires experience on your part to know when a certain disease is likely to strike.

Fungicides are toxic and should be handled like all other hazardous materials and pesticides. Follow the label directions exactly and never reuse fungicide containers for any other purpose. If you have questions or concerns over the use of the fungicides, check with your local lawn center expert.

Anthracnose
Colletotrichum graminicola

Black spots form in warm, moist weather. Grass turns yellow, brown. Control: Maneb and zinc sulfate, benomyl, chlorathalonil or thiophanate-methyl and mancozeb.

Fairy ring
Marasmius oreades

Ring of dark-green grass or mushrooms around dying grass. Control: No fungicidal control. Hide with high-nitrogen fertilizer.

Fusarium patch
Fusarium nivale

(Pink snow mold) Tan or pinkish 2–8 in. spots with web-like threads. Control: Benomyl, mancozeb, iprodione or thiophanate. Avoid high-nitrogen fertilizers.

Leaf spot

Helminthosporium species

Kentucky bluegrass grows brown circles on leaf until entire blade withers. Control: Anilazine, captan, iprodione or mancozeb.

Pythium blight

Pythium species

(Grease spot, cottony blight) Attacks new lawns. Blades turn greasy black. Control: chloroneb, metalaxyl or propamocarb.

Powdery mildew

Erysiphe graminis

Dust of whitish-gray patches cover grass blades. Control: benomyl, cycloheximide or triadimefon.

Red thread

Corticium fuciforme

(Pink patch) Bright pink threads kill grass in patches. Control: anilazine, iprodione, mancozeb or triadimefon. Fertilize with nitrogen.

Rust

Puccinia species

Rust-colored patches wipe off. Control: anilazine, chlorothalonil or triadimefon. Fertilize with nitrogen.

Slime mold

Physarum cinereum

Light to violet-blue 1–24 in. mass occurs suddenly in warm weather. Chemical controls are usually not necessary. Rake up.

Stripe smut

Ustilago striiformis

Black stripes on grass blades. May split and kill leaves. Control: thiophanates or triadimefon

Patch problems

Brown, Fusarium, and Ophiobolus patch—dollar spot—necrotic ring spot: patches of dead grass. Control: benomyl or triadimefon.

CARE PROBLEMS

SITE AND CARE

If your lawn's appearance is the problem, or it doesn't respond to treatments for pests and disease, the cause is usually care or site. These include over-watering, mowing, or poor soil conditions.

Over-watering is the most common maintenance problem. Keeping turf moist all the time weakens grass and allows weeds, disease and pests to attack it. Water so the top 2 in. of the lawn dries out before soaking it again. Too little water also damages a lawn, leaving it weak and susceptible to pests and diseases.

Scalping the lawn with the mower damages or kills grass plants, but so will too-high growth. Each grass type should be mowed when it grows to one-third taller than its optimum height (see pgs. 36–37). Keep the mower blades sharp. Dull blades will tear the grass and invite infection by fungal diseases, rather than cut it.

Dethatching and aerifying the turf at regular intervals are also important to healthy lawns, as is proper fertilization.

Sometimes, though, the problems are even more complex and may involve your specific site. For example, a large shade tree may rob your lawn of needed sunlight and water, or your soil may be too acidic. Or, on hillsides, water may run off too quickly to soak into the soil. Such sites appear to have blotchy, green areas intermingled with dry or dead spots.

In colder parts of the country, the high mineral content from snow melt or road deicing salt sometimes causes problem. If you think that may be the case in your area, check with your local lawn center expert to recommend a special grass mixture that can tolerate salts.

Bare Spots
Bare spots on new lawns. Seed has not sprouted. Causes include lack of water, acidic soils or low soil temperature.

Unrooted Sod
Sod fails to root. Re-roll, water until thoroughly saturated.

Scalped Areas
Caused by mower sinking into thatch or high spots. Dethatch or level by adding sand and topsoil to low spots.

Salt Accumulation
Dead spots near streets salted during winters. Soak thoroughly and often to flush salt from soil.

Compacted Soil
Starves turf by blocking nutrients and water. Aerify (see pgs. 38–39) regularly.

Drought
Choose drought-tolerant grass in drought areas.

Shade
Turf doesn't grow well in shade. Prune trees, or select shade-tolerant grasses.

Over-watering
Most common lawn problem. Too much water weakens plants, allows attack by pests, weeds and diseases. Causes shallow rooting.

SPECIAL CARE
TREES AND LAWNS

LEAVES

Raking leaves can be enjoyable and will help your lawn's health. Raking reduces the risk of damaging lawn diseases, insects and other pests. Leaves provide shelter for these unwanted visitors and prevent light and water from reaching the grass. As they decompose, they steal nutrients and air from the grass roots.

SHADE-TOLERANT GRASSES

Choosing the right grasses for your lawn requires thoughtful planning if the site includes shade trees. Choose grasses that will grow in shaded conditions. Imagine your trees' size in several years when you pick your grasses. Ask your garden store for advice on grasses developed for shady areas.

CARE TIPS

Although tree trunks seem sturdy and tough, they are delicate. When trees are cut by mowers, trimmers or other power equipment, these injuries permit insects and diseases to get past the protective bark and into the tree. Don't use string trimmers near tree trunks—their flailing strings quickly girdle and kill. Avoid shallow watering, too—surface roots will become large and unsightly.

TREES AND LAWN CARE

Lawns that contain trees or large shrubs require special attention. By shading the lawn and blocking the rain, trees and shrubs may rob the lawn of needed water, sunlight and nutrients. Tree leaves, if not raked from the lawn, often provide homes for pests and diseases. Evergreen trees may cause the soil to become too acidic. With a little care and planning, you can have wonderful shade trees and a beautiful lawn, too.

The biggest problem most trees cause for your lawn is shade. Most grasses do not grow as well without full sunlight. One way to solve the problem is to trim the tree or tall shrub to allow at least half of the sunlight to filter through. This can be done by carefully selecting the branches to be cut so the tree isn't disfigured. A second step you may want to take in shaded areas is to plant grass types that grow well without full sunlight. You can also reseed every year under trees using annual or perennial ryegrass. Another solution, of course, is to cut the tree or shrub out entirely; but if you value the tree and its shade, pruning or planting shade-tolerant grasses is a better way to go.

If you are planning your lawn and landscape, remember that deciduous trees that lose their leaves in winter provide excellent summer shade, but also require more work in autumn. Their leaves should be raked within a few days of falling because they provide pests and lawn diseases with perfect homes.

Evergreen trees, such as pines, don't present a leaf problem except for falling needles, but they can change your soil's acid-alkaline balance. Test your soil periodically and add lime when needed.

FALL LAWN CARE

Pre-winter lawn care includes fertilizing,
dethatching, aerificating, raking, overseeding,
mower maintenance and controlling pests. Most
grasses grow slowly as winter approaches, but
root development continues. Dethatch your lawn,
then apply high phosphorus and potassium
fertilizer. It's the best time to seed or overseed
lawns.

Cold Climates

First Mow to normal height. Apply high phosphorus/potassium fertilizer during autumn's first cool nights.

Then Rake leaves to keep lawns healthy by removing debris that block water and nutrients while harboring pests and diseases.

Last If necessary apply fungicides and insecticides to control diseases and bugs. Follow label directions.

Warm Areas

First Mow warm-season grasses such as bermudagrass in the fall and fertilize with balanced fertilizer.

Then Overseed dormant warm-season grasses with perennial ryegrass to keep the lawn green all winter long.

Last Keep lawn moist by watering overseeded areas until all ryegrass germinates.

Lawn Care Calendar
Pacific Northwest

Kentucky bluegrass, bentgrass, fine fescues and perennial ryegrass grow well in the cool, moist climate of the Pacific coast, Northwest and British Columbia. Soils vary, but tend from acidic in the north to alkaline in the south.

January
Apply moss control agents as required. Check for lawn diseases and treat as required.

February
Lawn and soil insects begin to hatch in southern zones. Red thread and rust disease peak in coastal areas, powdery mildew and fusarium patch in mountains. Apply fertilizers with potassium and phosphorus.

March
If temperatures are over 60° F, apply high-nitrogen fertilizer and pre-emergent weed controls to prevent annual weeds. Reseed bare spots.

April
Peak of grass growth season. Apply high-nitrogen fertilizer and broadleafed weed controls. Prevent insect infestations by inspecting and controlling outbreaks.

May
Grass growth slows. Water if rainfall does not provide enough moisture. Control grassy weeds by hand, broadleafed weeds with selective controls.

June
Fertilize and water if rainfall does not provide enough moisture. Continue weed control measures. Inspect for lawn insect infestations and control.

July
Water at least 1 in. per week to provide deep roots with moisture. Fertilize with high-nitrogen fertilizer.

October
With the beginning of winter rains, turfgrasses begin to grow rapidly. Mow, apply fertilizer that is high in nitrogen and phosphorus to prevent soil exhaustion and promote strong root growth.

August
Water at least 1 in. per week. Continue weed and insect control measures.

November
Temperatures cool. With heavy rains, lawn diseases may become a problem. In northern coastal areas, moss may also grow. Apply fungicides and moss control agents, as necessary.

September
Do soil test. Dethatch and aerify if thatch buildup and soil compaction are a problem. Reseed bare spots, mulch with peat moss and water so that grass is well established before winter rains.

December
Continue regular mowing. Fertilize as long as grass continues its rapid seasonal growth and temperatures climb over 60° F.

Lawn Care Calendar
The Southwest

Bermudagrass, buffalograss, dichondra and zoysiagrass are choices for warmer areas, while improved Kentucky bluegrass and turf-type tall fescues do best in cooler sections. Soils are generally alkaline and require treatment with iron supplements for best results.

January
Mow, water and check for lawn diseases or insect infestations. Treat as required.

February
Reseed bare spots with warm-season grass, water so that grass is well established before hot weather arrives. Apply fertilizers with iron, potassium and phosphorus.

March
Apply high-nitrogen fertilizer to help warm-season grasses out of dormancy. Apply pre-emergent weed controls. Check for soil insect infestations and apply controls if necessary. Mow regularly.

April
Warm weather. Peak of warm-season grass growth season. Apply high nitrogen fertilizer and broadleafed weed controls. Prevent insect infestations by inspecting and controlling outbreaks.

May
Water if rainfall does not provide enough moisture. Control grassy weeds by hand, broadleafed weeds with selective controls. Allow grass to grow 1/2 in. taller to conserve moisture and vigor.

June
Continue watering. Continue weed control measures. Inspect for lawn insect infestations and control them. Mow grass 1/2 in. taller.

July

Continue watering. Water at least 1 in. per week to provide deep roots with moisture. Fertilize with high-nitrogen fertilizer. Mow grass 1/2 in. taller.

October

Seasonal dormancy of warm-season grasses begins in cooler parts of the region. Overseed with perennial ryegrass, fertilize and mulch with peat moss for lush winter lawns.

August

Water at least 1 in. per week. Continue weed and insect control measures. Mow grass 1/2 in. taller.

November

Dormancy of warm-season grasses continues. Temperatures cool and winter rains begin. Lawn diseases may become a problem—apply fungicides as necessary. Water through dry spells.

September

Do soil test. Dethatch and aerify if thatch buildup and soil compaction are a problem. Apply iron-supplement fertilizers.

December

Dormancy of warm-season grasses continues. Mow overseeded perennial ryegrass. Fertilize every 4–6 weeks with high-nitrogen fertilizers.

Lawn Care Calendar
Northern Midwest and Central Canada

In this cool region, Kentucky bluegrass, hard fescues and creeping red fescue, or mixtures, are best. Soils range from alkaline and sandy to acidic and clay—soil tests are important for good results.

January
Lawns are dormant.

April
Grass begins to grow. Fill in low spots and reseed bare areas. Apply high-nitrogen fertilizers, soil insect controls. Check for cool-season diseases, such as fusarium patch.

February
Lawns remain dormant.

May
Peak of spring grass growth. Apply pre-emergent weed controls. Check for disease and insect infestations. Mow grasses 1/2 in. lower to encourage growth.

March
On mild days in southern areas, rake any autumn tree leaves or plant debris that may still be present. Aerify if not done in autumn.

June
Continue disease and insect control inspections. Apply broadleafed weed controls, if necessary. Mow and fertilize with high-nitrogen fertilizer. Watering should be flexible, depending on rain.

July

Water if rain is insufficient. Mow. Continue weed and insect control inspections.

October

Grass growth slows. Rake autumn leaves from turfgrass surface to prevent disease and insect pest infestations. Stop fertilizing, but water regularly until ground freezes.

August

Water and mow as required. Continue weed and insect control measures. Control broadleafed weeds if necessary.

November

Lawns begin winter dormant period. Remove autumn leaves and plant debris before snow covers turfgrass. In warmer climates, apply antifungal agents to prevent disease.

September

Grass begins autumn growth. Do soil test. Dethatch and aerify if thatch buildup and soil compaction are a problem. Apply fertilizer and mow 1/2 in. lower to promote strong growth.

December

Lawns are dormant.

Lawn Care Calendar
The South

The most recommended grass is bermudagrass, with bahiagrass, carpetgrass, centipedegrass and zoysiagrass for special areas. Cool-season grasses, including bluegrass, perennial ryegrass and tall fescue, are successful in higher elevations. Soil is variable—do a soil test.

January
Reseed bare spots with warm-season grass, water so that grass is well established before weather warms. Apply fertilizers with potassium and phosphorus.

February
Mow, water and check for lawn diseases or insect infestations. Treat as required. In deep South, apply high-nitrogen fertilizer to shock warm-season grasses out of dormancy.

March
Apply high-nitrogen fertilizer to help warm-season grasses out of dormancy in northern-tier states. Check for soil insect infestations and apply controls if necessary. Mow regularly.

April
Warm weather begins. Apply pre-emergent weed controls. Continue applications of high-nitrogen fertilizer. Prevent insect infestations by inspecting and controlling outbreaks.

May
Peak of warm-season grass growth. Water if rainfall does not provide enough moisture. Control grassy weeds by hand, broadleafed weeds with selective controls.

June
Continue watering as needed. Continue weed control measures. Chinch bugs and sod webworms peak—inspect for infestations and control insect pests.

July

Continue watering as needed. Fertilize again with high-nitrogen fertilizer. Control weeds, insects and diseases.

October

Do soil test. Apply lime or sulfur if pH becomes too acidic or alkaline. Dethatch and aerify if thatch buildup and soil compaction are a problem.

August

Continue weed and insect control measures. Mow and water as needed.

November

Seasonal dormancy of warm-season grasses begins in cooler parts of the region. Overseed bermudagrass with a fine-leafed perennial ryegrass for lush winter lawns.

September

Continue disease, weed and insect control measures. Mow and water as required.

December

Dormancy of warm-season grasses continues. Lawn diseases may become a problem—apply fungicides as necessary. Mow overseeded ryegrass. Fertilize every 4–6 weeks with high-nitrogen fertilizers.

Lawn Care Calendar
Northeast and Maritime Canada

Bluegrass and bluegrass mixtures with fine fescues and perennial ryegrass are the most common and successful turfgrasses. Soils are generally acidic and require periodic treatments with garden lime for lush, green lawns.

January
Lawns are dormant.

April
Grass growth begins in cool regions. Fill in low spots and reseed bare areas. Do soil test. Apply lime and high-nitrogen fertilizers, soil insect controls. Check for cool, moist diseases, such as fusarium patch.

February
Lawns are dormant.

May
Peak of spring grass growth. Apply pre-emergent weed controls. Check for disease and insect infestations. Mow grasses 1/2 in. lower to encourage growth.

March
Lawns are dormant.

June
Continue disease and insect control inspections. Apply broadleafed weed controls if necessary. Mow and fertilize with high-nitrogen fertilizer. Watering should be flexible, depending on rain.

July
Water if rain is insufficient. Mow. Continue weed, disease and insect control inspections.

October
Grass growth slows. Rake autumn leaves from turfgrass surface to prevent disease and insect pest infestations. Stop fertilizing, but water regularly until ground freezes.

August
Grass begins second seasonal growth. Fertilize with high-nitrogen fertilizer and mow 1/2 in. lower to promote strong growth. Water as required. Control broadleafed weeds if necessary.

November
Lawns become dormant. Remove autumn leaves and plant debris before snow covers turfgrass. In warmer climates, apply antifungal agents to prevent disease.

September
Weather cools. Dethatch and aerify if thatch buildup and soil compaction are a problem. Continue disease and insect control inspections.

December
Lawns are dormant.

Lawn Care Calendar
Rockies and Mountain

Bluegrass is the chief turfgrass for higher elevations, although mixes with fescues and perennial ryegrass are popular where winters aren't too harsh. Soil is generally shallow, with drainage problems. They require frequent fertilizing and iron supplements.

January
Lawns are dormant.

February
Lawns remain dormant.

March
Lawns remain dormant.

April
Grass begins to grow in warmest areas. Remove autumn tree leaves or plant debris on mild days. Fertilize with a high-nitrogen fertilizer containing iron.

May
Grass growth begins in cool regions. Fill in low spots and reseed bare areas. Do soil test. Apply high-nitrogen fertilizers, soil insect controls. Check for cool, moist diseases, such as fusarium patch.

June
Peak of spring grass growth. Apply pre-emergent weed controls. Check for disease and insect infestations. Mow grasses 1/2 in. lower to encourage growth.

July

Continue disease and insect control inspections. Apply broadleafed weed controls, if necessary. Mow and fertilize with high-nitrogen fertilizer. Watering should be flexible, depending on rain.

October

Grass growth slows and lawns become dormant. Rake autumn leaves from turfgrass surface to prevent disease and insect pest infestations. Stop fertilizing, but water regularly until ground freezes.

August

Grass begins second growth cycle. Fertilize with high-nitrogen fertilizer and mow 1/2 in. lower to promote strong growth. Water as required. Control broadleafed weeds if necessary.

November

Remove remaining autumn leaves and plant debris before snow covers turfgrass. Where winters are mild, apply antifungal agents to prevent turf diseases.

September

Weather cools. Dethatch and aerify if thatch buildup and soil compaction are a problem. Continue fertilizer applications, disease and insect control inspections.

December

Lawns remain dormant.

LAWN CARE CALENDAR
MID ATLANTIC-
TRANSITION STATES

A transition zone between the cool, humid North and the hot, humid South, with a wide variety of soils and microclimates. Local advice is best in choosing turfgrass types, although cool-season grasses such as turf-type tall fescues are most common and popular. A soil test is very important.

January

In cool areas, grasses remain dormant. Some spring growth may begin in warmest areas of the region.

February

In warmer areas, reseed bare spots with warm-season grass. If rainfall is limited, water so that grass becomes well established. Apply fertilizers with potassium and phosphorus.

March

Spring growth begins. Do soil test. Reseed as necessary. Apply high-nitrogen fertilizer to promote strong growth of cool-season grasses, shock warm-season grasses out of dormancy. Mow frequently, water and check for lawn diseases or insect infestations.

April

Warm weather begins in southern areas. Apply pre-emergent weed controls. Apply high-nitrogen fertilizer. Prevent insect infestations by inspection and control. Cool-season grass growth peaks.

May

Warm weather reaches northern section. Peak of warm-season grass growth. Water if rainfall does not provide enough moisture. Control grassy weeds by hand and broadleafed weeds with selective controls.

June

Continue watering as needed. Continue weed control measures. Insect hatch peaks—check for infestations and control any outbreaks.

July

Continue watering as needed. Fertilize again with high-nitrogen fertilizer. Control weeds, insects and diseases.

August

Continue weed and insect control measures. Mow and water as needed. Cool-season grasses begin second seasonal growth period. Fertilize and mow.

September

Weather cools. Continue disease, weed and insect control measures. Mow and water as required.

October

Do annual dethatching and aerification if thatch buildup and soil compaction are a problem. Remove fallen leaves and plant debris from turfgrass to prevent disease and insects.

November

Seasonal dormancy of warm-season grasses spreads to warmer climate areas. Remove fallen leaves.

December

Lawns are dormant in all but mild coastal areas.

LAWN CARE CALENDAR
TROPICAL AND
SEMI-TROPICAL

In areas where winter temperatures seldom fall below freezing, bermudagrass is popular. Other warm-season grasses, including zoysiagrass, St. Augustinegrass and carpetgrass are also popular. Soil conditions may vary, and a soil test is important for lawn care.

January
Plug or reseed bare spots in bermudagrass lawns, then water so that grass is well established before weather warms. Apply fertilizers with potassium and phosphorus.

April
Peak of warm season grass growth. Mow and fertilize. Prevent insect infestations by inspecting and controlling outbreaks. Control grassy weeds by hand, broadleaf weeds with selective controls.

February
Do a soil test. Apply high nitrogen fertilizer to shock warm season grasses out of dormancy. Mow, water and check for lawn diseases or insect infestations. Treat as required.

May
Water if rainfall does not provide enough moisture. Mow and fertilize. Check for diseases and insect infestations.

March
Warm weather begins. Apply pre-emergent weed controls. Check for soil insect infestations and apply controls if necessary. Mow and fertilize regularly.

June
Continue watering as needed. Continue weed control measures. Inspect for insect infestations and control diseases.

July

Continue watering as needed. Fertilize again with high nitrogen fertilizer. Control weeds, insects and diseases.

October

Perform annual dethatching and aerification if thatch buildup and soil compaction are a problem.

August

Continue weed and insect control measures. Mow and water as needed.

November

Seasonal dormancy of bermudagrass begins in cooler parts of the region. Overseed bermudagrass with perennial ryegrass for lush winter lawns.

September

Continue disease, weed and insect control measures. Mow and water as required.

December

Dormancy of bermudagrass continues. Lawn diseases may become a problem—apply fungicides as necessary. Mow overseeded ryegrass. Fertilize every 4–6 weeks with high nitrogen fertilizers.

LAWN CARE TOOLS

Caring for your lawn is easy if you use the right tools. Expensive power equipment, used just once in a while, should be rented from a nearby equipment rental yard. A home gardener should have most of these essential items in their toolshed or shop.

Hoe

Hand edger

Water hose

Lawnmower

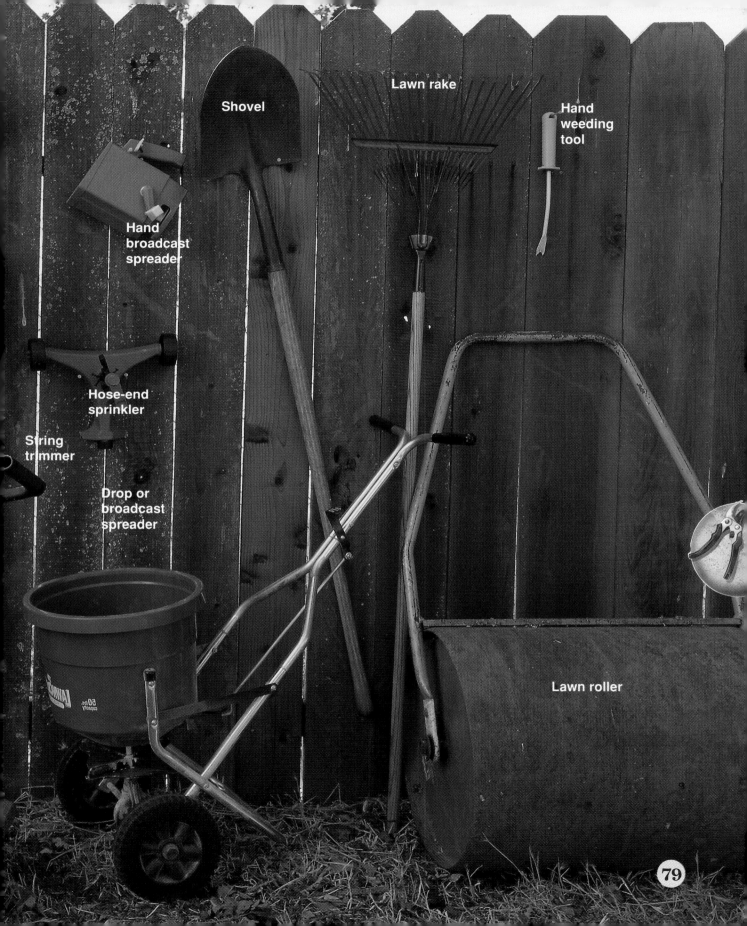

Shovel

Lawn rake

Hand weeding tool

Hand broadcast spreader

Hose-end sprinkler

String trimmer

Drop or broadcast spreader

Lawn roller

A Note From
NK Lawn and Garden Co.

For more than 100 years, since its founding in Minneapolis, Minnesota, NK Lawn & Garden has provided gardeners with the finest quality seed and other garden products.

We doubt that our leaders, Jesse E. Northrup and Preston King, would recognize their seed company today, but gardeners everywhere in the U.S. still rely on NK Lawn & Garden's knowledge and experience at planting time.

We are pleased to be able to share this practical experience with you through this ongoing series of easy-to-use gardening books.

Here you'll find hundreds of years of gardening experience distilled into easy-to-understand text and step-by-step pictures. Every popular gardening subject is included.

As you use the information in these books, we hope you'll also try our lawn and garden products. They're available at your local garden retailer.

There's nothing more satisfying than a successful, beautiful garden. There's something special about the color of blooming flowers and the flavor of home-grown garden vegetables.

We understand how special you feel about growing things—and NK Lawn & Garden feels the same way, too. After all, we've been a friend to gardeners everywhere since 1884.